UDP :: DOSSIER

*distance decay*
© 2015 by cathy eisenhower

Distributed to the trade by
SPD / Small Press Distribution
spdbooks.org

ISBN 978-1-937027-52-0
First Edition, First Printing

Ugly Duckling Presse
The Old American Can Factory
232 Third Street #E-303
Brooklyn, NY 11215
uglyducklingpresse.org

Supported in part by a generous grant from the
National Endowment for the Arts

*distance decay*

*distance decay*

cathy eisenhower

1. *distance decay*  11

2. *genogram*  49

3. *personality theory*  67

4. *welcome back*  87

1.
*distance decay*

Rape-supportive attitudes, endorse me —

then claim a vast face
confiding its entitlement to forced intercourse.


looking hard without ocular support,
pretending to have a weapon, looking, a
blouse alpha, an I subscale, a genital
validity

the desire to harm an object with an object.

the desire to clock distance from the home to the offense.

index a fear of rape
kurtosis meaning bulging blunts the measure:
penetration with a finger
penetration of a face or of a scar
penetration with a peakedness in foul paper

how does one spatially behave without

check in this logarithmic transformation on the slit
& verbal threats rehinged with erotemes & white
will others migrate south of this hole to feed on waste
butterfly their names, assume the shape of
broken histograms

there is a type of fucking it desires to see
amid some real or abstract fields of kindling
made inaudible underfoot by the folds of gray cloth
so close to the ear & touching swollen skin

before there was light
 —and detach expressions of satisfactions from them, is that broken?


you don't have to write about rape
if you want to ...

you don't have to write about writing about rape
if you have to ...

you don't have to rape
to not write about it ...

as the need for reference
surfaced, as the soil however
willing borne, end
with a likeness


lustrous cunning, the bed,
(two beds), if you want to (what)
mirror the manner of
head-free tongue, Cervantes


candling, a public alone,
pulling off the little part
their floatings were mantles
inside themselves

cankered ask
is to rust
as mere is
to nation

the clean body conducting some
times would rip

the first rape ever happened yester on the
window highway, laying
such tools as statements & fragments & crotch mints down
as hard furniture to hardly couch
the dedicated act.

from how it came about, the similarities are not worth
elaborating.
                        desire
to put oneself in relation to history through violence —
I feel so connected to whomever, then.

"the" waits for it.
metaphors for burning.
the burning.

one stands around the stove heating forks in the flame.
one thinks that one sees it in person, anima verging on guess.
an invisible slathers known items with sweet.
nothing in no one will touch the dwellings
curiously, capillary home, you grow that giant
photo on the door to ripe, unfeeling there.

anamorphic canine teeth appear on this line
eligible weapons wrought in glad mouths.
"our hair" is on the roof and on the floor
"our heads" set fire to them.

the quoted hymns & choirs come undone
whose love for blouse denied nay reconciled
the struggle with captive reruns of birds

"[I] was trying to sell [her] cleaning supplies,
and then [I] raped [her]."
"[I] tried and tried to sell the supplies."

save the rape on time
in a secret buoy
ranging through ranges of minutes —

of them heaps Perhaps

scan defining
ran raining up
up to the vitals

by the term man they mean

hardly a gang rape goes by
there's not an itching brain

stupid jar day

those structures running through
speaking naked in which the fact

of speech surrounds
that rape artist

did you contemplate it/did it/someone/was it/when

was no the double — sum of words
here once dismissed by which you've
worked the finger up
italics drawn from plastic fruit

p. 499 — the internal stranger describes
the dead descriptions, predicts
distances from untoward yours
to n=3, it was not said in saying yours

it was not figures drew two doors together
as a function of past 19s, & grateful dead
to question cat-faced stone above that coming
supremer dog which kept the face unpublished

petting neck this hard to motile statement
fuck romantic knowledge,
comic findings, clown-faced clasp or narrow clown
projected onto cock withdrawing

how many cleavings say they've not been raped,
what are their addresses,
in answer the boundless subsequence of if
there were a spanish mattress, caryatid

in the background, urgent, urgent being in the feeling
of a six, curled physical fragment — of flesh, still
shopping for details of your painful nest

who cannot stop raving this which
let me shame the ears with hearing
hardly what was felt on the bareness
of back to brain & back & then not backing.

attempts to recollect the infinite end
in raving, begin in being raved severally
refusal makes a title of the body: how
to strike out when you prepare to leak.

the mumble is coated with hours on end
the pipes transporting fire to herself at rest
then some abstraction breaks or sprouts a field
more likely it doesn't

this sipping makes the day a structure
familiar shaken smile over the drink
as to rave quietly from warm dangers

to splinter the raping into sponsorships
with which to rub this cornea via eyelid
pushing grit to the edge to help it escape
hey hi, i'm writing a poem

grit is feetless not to say legless
floating toward a crease
instead of listing withholdings
i'm writing a poem

the crease stands in for the stand-in
when provisions get scarce, difficult stuff changes its status
to more or less difficult, we don't need you now
it's become so easy that safely we facts enjoy our paychecks

to deposit the moneyroll into my pocket
which sings through cloth skin and muscle into hip flexor
vagina is ten percent of a pie chart
what color should it be for this presentation

for now, remote and dead you dip the walls
into walls the shades of cock solely rent, or meaning

if I didn't dream my rapist in my in
stopping to share small rooms with me
to dip "dreamt" into speechless acts

or, where once was mouth
(it is all mouth as photos found in lower quadrants),
the dead field of faceness

that everyone faces the ground on the ground
that abstractly sat candled remained perforated scram-bled

"i want you to rape this much"
forcefully
on the ground
your stump the bad of a bird's head

puzzling machine elegance
into unnamed injections and thighs
completing might with might

arm us with seamless
implementations, cornmeal claiming the function
of eyes, muddy teeth

the out of feeling

the out of manual judgment

the swallowing out of it

The inevitability of death tinges everything of the toast green,

which causes anger to also rise up in the toast,

perhaps another color beneath the one,

and the number 9.

My rapist lives in Seattle.

He won an award last year, or, several years from now, will have.

His telling of his past must look like fine-tuning a radio.

That's what I will be, a man fine-tuning a radio.

Finger gestures misplace hyphens to indicate fully rejected still lifes.

After his name—one of many Richard ▮▮▮▮—a comma.

Richard ▮▮▮▮ received the ▮▮▮▮▮▮ Award for ▮▮▮▮▮▮.

I do not want to push this information into you,

however nowhere soft and warm to put it appears before you appear.

"In a ▮▮▮▮▮ understanding can be hard to find, these award winners ▮▮▮ served ▮▮▮▮▮▮▮▮ the community ▮▮▮▮▮▮▮▮▮▮▮▮ effective communication," said ▮▮▮▮▮▮▮, president of ▮▮▮▮▮▮▮.

When you ask yourself or your neighbor what you want from your feelings
> (go ahead)

then you can hear the individual strains of traffic,

their pitches and textures,

construct litanies of delinquent comparisons as a treat.

When you are not raging me, I am not considering not raging you.

From want of speechlessness and also from being in it.

What my structure is is this loom toward analysis.

If staring wild at vector shadows launched from a live source of mouth light
can extract loving heads that nuzzle from inside the body walls,
then what else could it possibly fucking want.

Whose mind has entered a man as hands full of diffident countries,
        font-shaped.

It holds lament patiently in its arrows.

This is the way we eyes clear the entering.

But the more I make of force as peer, the stranger I am dreamt.

That I belong to it of body-colored ink, a mineral year.

I try to be discursive. Miraculous.

we feel like socially it wants the words to notice me,
said the words on the white wall.

it was my whom, that expanse, all numbers swallowed for better radiance.

be holding your cock when I come,
visible organ, killing your teeth as one by one
they startle the lip to violence, they discourse
over fresh remains.
near is dangerous to grasp said the wall to think
she founded instructions on her anti-retinal laze

then 2 escapes
                            sing softly-in-the-rape

& ran
when it saw
she's a man

rape is a great metaphor for rape when properly defined

the microscopic rape's travels called cold in wells, found & left

when you wants to be heard & be beheld

clamor to keep releasing eyes from mobile photos

cheek, cease, nation, blackface

& if keeps wanting me back there, unmet, mounted on the wall

he asked if lynching counts as violence

such feeling methods signal proof of the attachment to above, attempt to fuse body parts with parts of houses

one cannot tear oneself from the real door

the notionally dangerous & actually trivial
what you are

casually mechanical
causally significant

I took that to be a body part attached to a bloody breathing machine

how many of your right nows just peacefully bleed

long punless lingua comes caught seeming for your sake

description links you to your own face that face resembling being the
    whole system

they stuck a head out of undetectable fire

it was like a face that traveled from home to welcome — not burnt but
burning, in question marks, oppressed
by the melodrama of cauterization

I don't want to wash the filthy white floor
the sudden anonymous prefatory pain
a sudden anonymous trivial pain

array all the objects out of use to line their burning with pieces of this,
    forcing the treetop bird silhouette to voicemail

(as the pagans flocked to salem
that is to say meanwhile)

we find this news a birth rape    contretemps
it was eery jailed and very
you know burn mark instead of face
that looks sympathetically at the water

I measured his tear as it slid
down the leather cuff
that difficult procedure turned to facts
hastened to the rest of them

the thinking of being giving only stops
when the being giving begins
or the being taken ends or begins
meet me at the rape kit backlog

that could be an example
touching the tips of citizens
with the dark of the cellar
where mice nest

specific pointed-at rape in the rocket sent to moon

it tinies the simul-mouth

wanting to say "while" in the contrastive sense

while it all goes moon, it is all pitted white against
white, vision-free


defense mechanics comma digital exam
don't seem to belong
but the bees do seem to

we want real metaphorical flowers
up in there

neuro-there in the fancy boredom kept
by me and the ones resembling me

wooden tables claiming to mean underneath
or atop where one is slammed onto it

you do want to imagine your rape differently

the loud sounds that travel unexamined
through apartment space, the checkbook

that passes fear along to the unexamined
cure, so examined it seconds itself like this

and so we just start fucking dancing

create an email alert for raping
the fisty roses ad nauseum
my accommodation rots the eye out of
sad to feel what fields grow feebly
toward our waning

the faces of the roses pretend
to form faces on the dais
as I pretend to face-fuck the roses
with rulers and chicken feet

the tenses lock thyroids to scissored eyelids
pronouns turn floaters

this is all
review to the vowel
dropping down toward heavenly
must & the sneeze that
could save you

all the golden-
nesses made me better lessons
& from keeping lesions current, like this
lesion I am right now is right

thinking that possessive telling gets styles over
the border, the nipples straining toward some
concrete noun mouth, thus force
the micro-rape projected into said mouth open
while we leaning squinting pop collusively

I said some shit that should have
inflection knocked out of it
(A) small amount, mixture, the discriminating
power (of the test) goes down

throw a blue shirt over the cell camera
& beat the fuck out of him

phantasmatic apple of fucking not to say rayping
& I say quarterly of constructing it that
fails to cheer or assume

the bird something something thought to gently shock the lake
angels without doorknobs, lit by that the words will not
produce a gun or jackknife

these biggest whitest feelings float open into tines
the nib's tapered fingers, form each other by the slit
native wavelet caught in the passing face
though burst it considers my illustrated pasts as income
& they do, charting then gunning down the smile

it needs more liquid than others
except the olives
that blur the nature of agencies
panting press
distinction is convention
talking things, what we have imbued with the ability to
arise in storing sanitas
stemming & storing
or self-contained subsystems alter
but I think marketing is the presupposition
& rape is
somebody else is doing it
they get cut
all sorts of bad
things happen
who gets to decide what value is
for to realistically enlarge yourself
I have …. tense
describe your husband
bring dictionary
knows grammatical structures
read & understand
(both of us)
do/does/doesn't
   —in English—tell me about it

so hear city trumpets when we rape
ourselves as Mexican lights
& measure less than thunder-
birds, strike to skin over skull

that rape grows ordered, boring, gentle
lands reach driveways entre dwellings
which organ drives a quickening breeze
to the dirty part, the numb to weary wing

mental money flowed in the street
as they loving to gladly trumpet
muffling shirts in the hole
to shove a thistle deep, till the mouth beeps

the women on every facial corner, pleading for investments
analyze the wreck into pleasures
they felt a wing in the throats of them
she took their phones & let them leave

along the prescription river
the snow so deep it stirred their frozen packaged cunts
one was to stir one with a stick yet
no event comes

that containment team in the rain caked raw with raping. *o sea* the need for letters spelling out white on on on the happy — little love rivulet gone to cake down the leg made of running. the tools cannot carry me far enough to carry this embrasure far enough, and what put through it (it) but erotemes come salty in the boil. *o sea* in father love being a male none not even once to speak these years the way they will have been when we hands and mouths have recourse to be said and felt, in every other moment but this constant throat. the 90 tablets slipped clean into the transparent toward, as gravel faintly projected onto piled torsos. touching eyes to them, lying down under the hole, is there an under the hole, is being smearing into the funnel crawling with falling birds of any type.

were you to mean when saying rape instead of race.

the white describing nun and her fake rape assailant.

2-ton black man faking out the bodega with pussy orange sections and phantom bread decimated by thoughts you broadcast about the perimeter.

the skid of a freckle on the retina.

fat purple trauma outlined in white, exclamation point, of enormous powdery 2D teeth caught between sneers.

don't make me pull the toys out —

filthy snowbank on the east side as white as white can be with the wind all fucked up invisible.

like I have a mouth.

like there's a cock in it for now.

I used txt to snare *my rapist.*
My dad, *my rapist*. Grandpa leads police graduates · REJECT CHEATERS ·
I've declared everything I own — Mikey

I found a picture of *my rapist* on the engagements page

I'll never name *my rapist*

I don't know if I will ever stop seeing *my rapist*

I have been seeing *my rapist* face

Seeing *my rapist* on TV made me shudder

I saw *my rapist* in town the other day and when he saw me he ran away.

I saw the love in Christ's face, not just for me, but for *my rapist*.

Have *my rapist* arrested!

<u>My Friend is Friends with</u> *my rapist*

It makes me see *my rapist* from 16 yrs old - 36 years ago, really clear.

**I nailed *my rapist***
To *my rapist*, there are a few things I would like you to know

On I married *my rapist* Steve confronts a rapist

funadvice my boyfriend is *my rapist*

"*my rapist*" needs to be outed

*My rapist's* parents and probably *my rapist* are very likely to be there.

I'm actually on decent terms with *my rapist*.

See the Glog! Billie Joe-*My Rapist*: wowza | Glogster.

*My rapist* is about to get out of jail.

I just found out that *my rapist* is dead. Not only is he dead, but he ended up killing a lot of women.

Read *My Rapist* by *Brain*

*My rapist* is a monster
Who is ugly inside and out

I still love *my rapist* Dad

i love *my rapist* E-book edition
**think my sister is marrying *my rapist***

**Check out the Falling for *my rapist*'s twin brother!!! story and write some great stories of your own.**

**I love *my RAPIST'S*** baby; Rape victim:

<u>**My date rapist is on Facebook as a "person I might know"**</u> I want him to confess and admit he was wrong. Should I contact him?

I drove *my rapist* to police. That's life.

**Sorry, we can't find "i-talk-to-my-rapist.jxkjjcvs.com"**

*My rapist* wouldn›t take no for an answer. her 4 fans are probably her posting under false id's histrionic personality+ dismorphic body disorder

Does *my rapist* recollect raping me as often as I do?

if you're *my rapist* - i'm your assassinator

He had a very cushy lifestyle. His kids are in private colleges. He owns two very expensive cars and now hes wearing pink underwear (sheriff Joe Arpaio) and sleeping on a medal bed.

liberating pictures since 2004. Login or Sign up · Feedback. Pictures tagged as *"my rapist"*. page of 1. 0 0 0 0. *my rapist* comments.

Anyway, the rapist did his homework and looked up how to defend himself by giving a very detailed description of what happened that night but couldn't give details about the sex.

XD these are *my rapist eyes*

oh nein it's a ninja rapist D:

rapist •Trappist • harpist • tempest •escapist, papist, rapist •landscapist • typist •misanthropist, philanthropist •aromatherapist, physiotherapist, psychotherapist, therapist

People have suggested "bring justice to *my rapist*" is really the same as:
- **put *my rapist* in jail** - 0 fewer people
- **Get A Life** + 766 more people
- **kill** + 297 more people

"Oh, I have to go forgive *my rapist*s."

She came over because she knows *my rapist* has attention deficit disorder and has a hard time focusing especially when he is scared. She stated she was afraid it would look like he was being uncooperative with PD when he wasn't intentionally acting that way.

*My rapist* agreed to complete a written statement however ex-girlfriend wrote the statement because *my rapist* stated he could not write it due to his handwriting not being legible.

I would marry *my rapist*, because it's God's will.

I would marry *my rapist* because he's very well hung.

Well I'm a Christian and I think this quote is not valid... Only the things I want to be valid are valid.

Rapists need the most love.

Would you marry your rapist? The Bible says its a good idea!
Christians love to quote Bible, so I thought I will as well.

Deuteronomy 22:28-29 (King James Version)

28If a man find a damsel that is a virgin, which is not betrothed, and lay hold on her, and lie with her, and they be found;

29Then the man that lay with her shall give unto the damsel's father fifty shekels of silver, and she shall be his wife; because he hath humbled her, he may not put her away all his days.

*My rapist* was never convicted. Did this mean I was less raped?

**A Cuddly Rapist.** *My rapist* wasn't a "great guy":

**I'll Have** *My Rapist* **With A Side of Cranberry Sauce.** As a vegan, I do not consume animals or their secretions.

*My rapist* spoke in tongues.

***MY RAPIST* IS A VERY FAMOUS CELEBRITY**

<u>**South Dakota: Where Rapists Live Forever!**</u>

as for causing myself & my arm, I take this space for gambit.

as for causing your personality to be my trauma, as it slowly thrives
       from dessication —

think to find an article alone hid among technique, among a gambit arm
       tattoo meant for throat, which functions as a decomposing screen.

that's a little too raped for complexity's sake.

if you say a positive trauma, then I will.

*2.*

*genogram*

I give you explanations
You give me experiences


There's no such thing as a baby
but that's what that is
your development is like a bowl of rocks
selected for their ugliness


I ordered a cheap polishing machine
from an infomercial
and gave it to your face
because I hate myself that much

it's like I'm the girl-baby in my cavity
because I am shiny there right now, delicious firelight
and also I want to kill people

I can't find the shiny in this
this item has been borrowed tangerine times
this ship of theseus a small invisible nut

*i've got a question:*
*do you like me?*

it's like a bag of wet pills has me,
or i have them
and shake my shiny at them

until the cooing drives its stakes
at some public event — a county fair
late in the county fair season
firefly on french fry in a symbolic
marriage of two types of shiny

wireless mutilation sucks out the micro-skeleton
enough that they hug for a long time and cannot stop hugging
the promise of health covers them in a color painful, yet shiny

mist each with a separate angel
use only infinitives to climb the trees
which will be on shiny fire

*identified patient*

that kind of yes intersection that I am,
your ocean discussion —
Hi Cathy, you are my friend.
I think you are, too, if I am thinking
correctly, as anything friend can make me feel
like I am into recording grief while also into
trying to make you my friend.
do you have any of those friends
that are like absurd surprising objects
pasted onto le petit chose?
I did, I do, one just went by — *hello* ... ?
hatred is the angel of the weak.
it is Feeling Week and so
feel with everyone at events until sunday.
this is too seductive to win.
i don't not like your experience. just not as
a document.

*mother #1*

i have to pee
because i am a baby
or you know what i mean
what looks like a pile of shit
on the cover
is a pile of it
i drew a circle of you
of you saying nothing words
of you mouthing nothing in a literal way
opening the mouth to stay closed
some found anger
this throttle of my organ
is a habit and is not real
you are dead but you are real
hair is cascading out of the dream
to silver the landlines
into one spatial hypothesis
jagged lines among you
mean fire and are fire

*mother #1*

flashbacks form the future
help the mountain climb us
inside big red dot
the mother of concepts contains
kissing you on your good mouth
excitedly mouthing cryptogrammic
melodies, like songs,
but not songs

bellied needles, as in
shoved into the belly
let us hear the height in her voice
the unreleased prototype
more verbose than this one
mothering like an actor
if this were a riddle
and she weren't the solution

*child #1*

I buried my burning in the cushion children
that ovoid vocal turning over the should table
and that is all that happens to a brain out in the weather
its bucket worn as a hat or a bracelet
imagining the feel of many guns to point
at the belly-up fish in its bowl
piping the buttercream script
*if you hert me I will cill you*
onto inedible surfaces

*father #1*

to reciprocate and lactate
        until the empathy gets personified by observers
come off as a tv personality —
        with special bathroom hair and things
coming off of the preferred substance,
        who ever who has it —
or come off it, as is inserted in
        the between space of awake and unconscious
for those who can't really ever
        really come off it

there is a square and it is full of meat
        then (then) yes then you (yes you) you remove the meat
from not just the square but from everywhere —
        from this everywhere brain
that shudder takes bodily form to continue itself
            (pass it down)
reproducing the breathing in of atrophy
        squeezed out under the truck tire

it keeps the killing on the plate
        a boy or a deer
meanwhile this permanent sadness
        clowning around the golf course
like a terrified clown with a club at a club
        cutting trunks with his putter
muttering about cutting up with his putter

        we don't want that now, as ever it has been
this not wanting of that, that, that, and that, and also that

daughter #1

radically negative species.
I spoke to myself all day, owned properties, linked power sources
to containment.
she spoke to herself all day
from the small insides of this label.
what was underneath was underneath nearest
the entrance and above, almost airborne, as well.
a desire to describe the ambient light
then kill it as required —
a filtered urge to reconstruct the ambient light
then burn it with a gun —
these we refer to pointedly, with pelvic discomfort,
as though the mall could exist
among the plight of chimps,
primate vagina full of sale racks,
the agent kiss[ ] (from one of the spectra of moments
not to be chosen here)
releasing milk into its vocal info,
~~penetrating data~~
~~with several organs.~~

*daughter #1*

~~(it feels it has to want to)~~

the circle full of mouths, they correctly
        shrunken to sizes of dust, seeming to be seen
that were put there, in the circle, to fill it —
        quantity of open, closed, somewhere between

to tamper with seeming till threatened with force
        a face predictably hot while scars fill with force
the edge of the screens flash messages
        when one holds something in one's hand and

and out of this these ropes tied from one
        to several stopwords, then tied to
human or plane then word again
        the net flung over the giant female statue's arm

you have a few goals you'd like to share
        in the form of monkeys and wire
the far step first into love, as a large number past
        the starch of brain ideas, lurching

like might come out of this, wash over acoustic
        kidney tremble where solid lines
are not solid lines but needles on the meter
        marking the tremolo, and the raw hand

~~(wrapped in a sock)~~

*father #1*

that razors scribble geometrics on the skin
        a pale froggy facial dysmorphia, & blood some

badness of form, the very pronoun of badness
        not causing the long slice to be felt or happening

coincident ladder, space between fingers, charity —
        room mysteriously required and requested

at times provided — he provided her partial face
        a lifetime explaining death to a child

a first foot lifted for spacing out the climb
        arms that swing and strike what's closest

*father #1*

and there are the stages, amorphously lit
       (escape before there is no escape)

it isn't clear where we ever were,
       at the rending, what was it?

medical tastes okay when the sparks fly up
       like "no receiving thoughts of his face"

*okay okay!*
what space stuck you inside it, where the blank round room
       scares blueness into kidneys

       how can color turn into an organ, out of simple fear, but it does

other organs hold the scent (of golden shag rug)
       hold the scent weeping over you

while you (or you) look to be slept and surgeried
       in the row of boxes of infants arrayed on the carpet

you drink yourself out of a bottle, love

you work yourself out of a general atmosphere, into an advancing figure

crawling through the legs of tunnels built of human legs —
       like certain blood is full of you, because it is

how to receive hands, in legs, or arms in mouths
    (in a fetal mood)

without particulate treason air — molecules climbing into your eye water
    burning you with treason fire

that feeling burning you while burning your likeness

*mother #1*

mass-produced instinct, wall of laws
and the psychic text
telling you to play games when you
were thinking "I should play
some games"
you were thinking, weren't you
that wall could not contain a being
placental constraint
as precursor to myths of screams
that denote animation

the crunching is filled with evening
damp salty mouth
while terminal dilation of passageways
terminates in half-filled-in circles
there is trouble discerning brown
from gold even with the legend
two pens touching on the table
she pulled up her family on the screen
it's like free-form chess
famished with people

being sea detective
or book of snow
what do I know
that knows me also

that this could be the final thing
to render all else
unnecessary — a killing of
the facial everything

glands puzzle through the items
as is being customary
stopping to explode
before just-turned backs

I honestly didn't hear
any cries for help
and the ones I hear
make me hope to be mine

disliking the echo of misnamed
relations trapped in my brainhome
fault of me also rhyming brain
with *in flagrante delicto*

*3.*
*personality theory*

when I practice parade fainting

also when I salt a caul

this sensation, my entire body field turned basket, prickle

the sac feeding the concept with concept, concept, concept, until, pop!

(there is resistance to formally labeling conceptualism as a mental disorder)

you may think this is a position.

fiber floating light light   light     lightlight lightlight lightlight lightlight

people cry snowflakes stainlessly
for these materials that I have

cast a type of play with no characters
just affliction-forged graphemes

enough white space to crawl out of
for desire to crawl out of

without feeling serifs draw blood
and also faintly feeling others feel them during the crawl

these materials that I have
repeat loadbearing, in a game of

finding the hole through us

I and fled a coming repetition
equivocally, seated in the viewing place

while this weather grows a personhood
over its century of uninterrupted stimuli

I waited as a house like everyone else's house has
where needing to be elsewhere requires

impediment just to admit it
protected from the harmless

an ottoman under the olive, there to forget to eat
and feel your face wearing off onto

whatever it mildly considers to be near
enough, the repeaters downed

flower pot
chariot
crow


it's all introductory to finding a dry child's mouth
disintegrating amid the violet
objects grown severely dry
until their objecthood harks vibrating bedside tables


the questions escape as remembrances
they want to float up but do not float up
in lieu of floating up
the substance breaks at release the substance wants
to shatter or flutter but next
to nothing occurs


I have nothing in my soul
I don't know nothing

digital has gone to me, many.

your love in one comes down waiting with mine,
matter of course, veiny,
that is a form of tubular life,
window as dressing (in the window).

it is not the dying
but the style of waiting,
crate of table of terror of feral digits
that would hone in on claws
to claws speak,
if there's a mouth around
to mouth some december.

i thought i should think of this for a long time,
as he is working the smear off a surface,
landscaped with oughts that we
of feeling use to thank the one
whose full solar blaze
(trees and grass, trees and grass)
await our sour science.

Even the full development of my personality is not enough. This full development must feel bad knowing my personality is not attractive bodybuilding. Do you think my personality is not fit for a relationship? I'm good looking, nice, etc., but my personality is like an empty box. Real Jesus, who he is, I desire you to know — I am an independent person, and my personality is not dictated by what these "spies" see in me, because I am a Jesus person set in stone, the hugging saint, as me and do self-forgiveness for defining myself as her — as I am one and equal as all personalities that exist. Is your favorite color a warm color or a cool color? Cool, but this personality is not like that. I hate how I can wear certain things because I have skin. I also would fail at their agency because my personality is not from Miami Beach. Skip & see how my personality is not the subject of your converted murderer, or play it safe and like that unlikeness, which really went above and beyond, just like my personality. So You Want To Be A Police Officer? Who doesn't? I might dye my hair, wear makeup, tan, spray pepper spray down my throat, but my personality is not extreme enough to be chosen as the protagonist of the really worthless and completely incompetent. I will take the personality of spurdaddy and leave on the drywall petroleum chariot. My personality is not right for me — it should find a department that's too mainstream and call me Shredded Jesus. My personality is not split, but fake, not equal, but reflective, not famous, but so super okay. My personality is not a sin, though reading it is like eating cookies. People think of military boot camp, because my personality is like military boot camp. It finds itself less anxious before my nude dates. It has such a high opinion of itself, what the feck? And you will now understand that my personality is not charismatic enough to draw crowds of people to it when I open my mouth. I think maybe my personality is not compatible with relationships. Note that my personality is also not tied up with my vagina. You have seen an example of my friend-making process throughout this essay.

personality sun, personality soon, personality lemon ice
with a little blood in it.
as I wipe myself
the functions come clear
through evalution, yes,
as through dollars, as though cast
in proprietary soft cartileges.

polishing the sink to an ex-
planet, its loose purple cock
full of more cock
sprouted out of the porcelain.

that is real personality.

how conscientious is your rooting —

how open are you to
experiencing the porcelain
on your least accessible flesh —
how stable are your
horsey tears and fears and rages —

we're all looking forward to working with what is now a permanent self

when I personify the personality, nothing happens

when I subjectivize it, the physical environment says
he hurt me in my pigeonhole

when I eat chicken out of the personality, I crave more chicken and less personality — I may even crave partial removal of the personality plus more chicken

whole persons explained what you were thinking

... me be, me be, me be
Be the good boy thief boy self, and starts ... with a ... with a p.
At least let her s-, ... know, gerontologically speaking,
about the occupation of stress by stress responses.

rethinking regarding housing system should first regard
my personality. I got a set of cues,
a 3D mental space and 7 emotions.

Note the touches and words of you on me,
my tissue needs,
which these ceilings make
anonymous.

We are experiencing a shortage —
of waffles due to a flood —
or due to the ego being a vampire —
the angels of death often use —
metaphors in order —
to get their point across —
they aren't closing —
they are angels of the death —
the most recent contributor to —
my swim through the sum water —
how is the ego —
shortage affecting you —
this —
this foods is making me stupid —
somehow forgive —
me and my development —
why did every commercial lie —
unskillfully to me —
why are the angels of death using —
metaphors to flood my ego —
with obstructions to peace? —
death comes on swift —
wings so please —
so join my club quick —
my ego is good with which —
my club will show you as it solves all —
the marital problems between me and your wife —

I'm indecisive about using —
around the angels of death —
who are very wise and cutting —
a place to bury during strangers —
during the flooding —
could be inside the angels —
those egos drip all time —
onto the very subjective representations of —
ourselves in crowds of others —
the manufacturing plants, utilitarianism, the question of the atomic —
these —
these burn the ego out —
of the physical body —
which is smoking salvia in a gaze upon Poussin's sylvan Arcadia —
tracing the real shadow of —
of its monkey mind —
about to make you hear what —
what can't be said —
as we get impotent in the bathroom mirror —
touch our faces to the stone —
that —
that is our fucking Everest now.

try to form your personality through:

- branding it with a love-shaped ember while finding a piece of eaten bread invisible in the metal can
- shaping the jaw muscle to a slipknot from mouthing the word please.
- banging chevrons to fine relations
- having a head for business
- saying your bruise is shaped like Africa
- ending with a repetition
- telling the world you are a prickly pear

um

whose head is happening —
when we want this poem to be
really important by the time
it's over

2 p.m. is starting right now
and so is my personality —
from scratch, and nut dust
possibly appropriate for snorting

I just want to lie down
and feel good for a while
for a while with foreground people
loving me methodically

sharp crumbs in the shape of
Huguenots stick to my skin
cause me to dream I am
Paul Revere

waving my styptic pencil
to clog a blood run
during the salt's froth and swell
on the flocculant face lugar

he never had the makings of a varsity athlete
he was like the appendectomy he never had
he never had the right farm equipment
he never had the blues before he wrote a poem based on The People of the State of California v. Eric Brown
he felt he never had the support of sugar ray
he never had the bleached blonde hair to give him nerve
it's as though he never had the footwork down, because he never did
he never had the father he never had
he never had the superior backing of this miracle
he never had the guts to tell you, and neither do I
he never had the courage to be excessively handsome, which takes more than courage, it takes a village full of ugly men for comparison
he never had the moment
he never had the plague, as far as he knew
he never had the comfort of a map
he never had the limp corrected
the big brother he never had discovered a secret cyber-underground of
    porn sites
he never had the luxury of a godmother diagnosis
he never had the discipline to add cardio to his toolbox — too bad
he never had the need to go anywhere because there was nowhere else
    to go
he never had the tackle numbers
he never had the impact on fine art of, say, Warhol
he never had the privilege of receiving any literary prizes
he never had the evil thoughts about destroying pop music
he never had the chance to confront the witnesses against him
he never had the radio on when he was driving
he never had the skills
he never had the stage to himself
he never had the slightest suspicion
he never had the opportunity to experience the slightest suspicion

she never had the chance to run
she never had the flu anyway
she never had the X
she never had the title or a corner office or she did but she couldn't want them
she never had the chance to relive prom
she never had the opportunity to return fire or take cover
She never had the stomach needles, so she drew on her limbs until satisfied that her skin was made to be covered in ink and not kisses
She never had the jack rabbit mantle
she never had the best thing in the end — irony
she never had the means to leave her spread wings
she never had the least affection for vows
she never had the dream to plant a vineyard or live on a farm
she never had the love of the common people
she never had the craving for Freud
she never had the operation
she never had the prosperous lifestyle that other children had
she never had the opportunity to have an opportunity
she never had the unconditional love of a parent
she never had the right to choose her own mate
she never had the body, the legs, or the style imagination to become a hero in the vast unknown
she never had the breakout hit to prove that he was lame
she never had the feelings, she never had the good old times
she never had the chance to be all she was cracked up to be
from that moment on, she never had the desire to binge or purge again
she never had the full sex change

ask me about my genitalia.

as if.

rising in an unmarked unsaid
mammal anger.

dressed as winter
& its analysis
hoping the stanching stanches.

body litter in the really real rain.

while conditions permit lying, dying, and crying
feloniously & also like sincerely.

good gates are like bad gates
in that they are gates.

Bitter, lovey, ghosty thoughts
written in the cake.

Desires aroused, as of wanting to care for others badly.

*4.*
*welcome back*

tiny tiny to small small

particulate lodged under veins sent to the surface where they poof etsplode

which hairs do the airs touche as they nasally pass themselves along poofing

I think terror can work for dessert if you pinch it hard enough then poof feel the sequence rattle you

removing so many I's from the email does not remove my narcissism but makes it more insidiously poooff

which came first is really a question of the second poofing

i think a tuft oh

and sat poof

which bore me tuffet-like

toward my small arena

lie across endful shards of glass

so small they are soft in ending

Welcome back.

1

2

3

4

now buy me a present.

no don't buy me a present.
I don't want any present at all.

I didn't mean that you should buy me this present
or any other type of present.

all the vagaries slide down the hill toward the center —

(what's for lunch?)

even in my dreams I'm distracted
by dream iPads playing movies
about baby dinosaurs stolen
from experimental swimming pools.

(what can I do?)
here's what I will say
to this one or that one
while there's anger in the water
poured into the other water

to make some amount of more or less
angry water.


the specific downfall of language related to liquid.

all the vagaries slide down the center
as though drinking a boring self
and pissing a boring self out.

the growling cycle follows into the something something sunset mind.

"I feel honored" to be in a landscape,
to be honored with a landscape named after a word
that I used to love.

sicker can't seems to red research

some stopping you are being

you are it all the more

saying feel while feeling thinking, or ends

typewritten intestinal dinner, singley said

i supplies a necessity

i feels lighter powder speaker

welling welling welling

                      feel hard at it

teeming skin




flames




scribbledy cared-for "M" over

the non-"M"


underlining a blue blotch

of particular characters



I can't seem to

                                    include

        *when you feel*



                         the red research



                 while thinking "loam"



                        Sick Powder Paradise



                                             awaits

                        brain sparkles feel



                                     lighter in the back

                                       seat, turn

green, cede


voice

more coffee to
practice observing the inside of this and that

when I make you feel something because I
don't want to feel it

when I feel you are making something because I
can't seem to make it

when you see something in my seeming to see
something about you that is leaking into the space
of your vibrations

the highest care is any type of touch

rinsing blood from cloth with water at the wrong temperature
while eating boiled eggs rubs me
half raw, correctly, with lack of killing in the background

I forget what is radical.
as though having a table makes you someone
crouching under a table

*pantograph*

some crimes you want to kill the landlord
or you are the landlord being killed & killing
while acting diagnostic, as anyone should
to be believed at the mental sea wall


otherwise you are building a new entrance
open onto unceasing cement
that I ridged with my tongue before they dried
enough to resist tampering


I don't have a refill indicator
also the one I have is ruined
enough to force profligate use of conjunctions
and the wearing of brooches pinned to the skin


and the ⊞ is pinned to your thigh
and drives along the wilder fuselage
and whatever crashed in the paper water
and we crouch by the wall, being drawn

that tearful state

resting, resting, over by the wayside

red metal shells, which one melts before drinking

one thinks to rotate  /  one thins to nightmare

there is always tinfoil among the pronouns

such very little sunspot swarm in the caruncula

awaiting neck scent, proximity

i see you i see you

Yesterday: I could not shit and thought of the day my mother would die and walked outside.

Every day: I wait listening to the air moving and watching the objects that move on account of it, and this is very poignant and moving in that parts of me inside shift into a peace.
Every day: You walk around and sit and speak and say you love me many times so that I can hear you and know it and have the words for myself.

Yesterday: texting the silence afforded me.
Sunday: The spokestiger in a nun's habit visited me during Doug's reading, infants in square bubbles hovering among the shining spines of my friends and the books of my friends and other fiendish strangers. At the time when the most rattling had stopped in the rows of bodies then real bubbles in the poems turned in the inside light cast by some of the words that were coming out of something both soft and hard, both here and already not here. I make that like is a feeling in the rows of rooms behind me clockwise, and you said twice that you once saw the man who sings deeply in the morning from the sidewalk.

Every day: I get literally pregnant.
Every day: I literally miscarry.
Wanting this to be better than I am
None of it metaphorical, in a car, the spasms of eviction ghosts on the sidewalk where belonging does not wait and is only for flashes of visions of moments between bodies who walk through the cotton covered in code for woman or man.

Yesterday: my thumb was too cold to end the call so I tucked the thumb into a nice warm noun.

I feel like making a poem right now after wiping myself clean, to lift my hood, to indulge in aphasic skirmishes, which certainly tells nothing of the tools we use to teethe on though I am reminded of those also. You are pulling chicken from a bone with your teeth close enough for all of my senses to have the capacity to experience this act multiply and at once, but some of the senses I select to be waiting.

Welcome back.

1

2

3

4

5

6

7

now buy me a present.

the homonymic is not very poignant at this point.

I want to speak about how I have changed
and how these words come out differently,
not as words, but as other beings, phenomena, etceteras.

but then I feel scared and know nothing,
which maybe is all.

this time I mean it.

it's a test isn't it —
it isn't a test of what "slough" means
in various social circles
such as this social circle,
the one you and I are.

this calls for a simile
but I would rather crack a tiny smile,
like this :).

*pantograph*

circle the dates of service in quiet shoes
speaking an English that will maybe be ok
to flash in the corner of the eyescreen
always refreshing sans feeling refreshed
or to spill out of another's brother hole


i'm not anything, like she said
while everywhere changing my name
to Guatemala Creeley
and then weeping uncontrollable cursors
from the water in my hands

having never heard of then, and paced
over the pine-dead fronds
ivy and weak weeds near the stump altar, weaving around
them as method of care, any method
on a bed of earth selected for its capacity
for walking in a weaving way while holding
a teaspoon to each eyeball, as I do, among others
who also walk further from the stump altar
than from their waking, or somewhere labyrinthine
toward a stump, many stumps at different times and
spots along with circular grasses confusing
the birds into household ghosts.

when everyone's future beautifully dies, I feel it
now in my skull, where water swells
in attempt to escape those organs
thought to manage ghosts of care.
How many stages? you may ask.
Five to seven.
What is the protocol? you may want to know.
But that isn't public.
I walked in thoughts that good emerged from caring
for crushed grasses, or to think that caring did
crush the grasses sexually, forgetting-then-remembering
to come back

one saying of it came
through carapace as mouth
visually cuddled the
square to infuse soft thought-
birds with the opposite
of stars (their many
opposites pouring from them —
overflown).
some like first-person
plural pronoun carefully erased
awakeness. avoid conjunction avoid
experiencing subtle films
of decay that is to search
mouth seam and eye seam
which at this time must always
move beside one — feel
a verb emerge so
physically through
the cavities feel it coat
learned alternatives sound bites,
lesion cavity walls create likeness
about them feel the wild
verb quake make histrionic sense of
all one's little powers.

scream
numb
lock
pause
insert

control to hibernate
control to break

to say the wanting of certain flocks of words to stop permanently existing. evening.

it shoved each letter into precision of stagger. desire to put precision again here down vast rectangles of relit dust.

under an unblown blanket.

where spell eradicated what counts as surface, axis, medicated lamp tucked away in the amorphous softness receiving it.

there is an unctuousness to this quality
when the flammable shoat-grunting humanity (as to time)
calms at the visual thigh, not that one — that one — yours — (pay attention)
perceived as an open letter to all
the animules in my condition, under my control
because imagined by my self and loved as such (also
real soft creatures)
the ointment upon your burning shoulder falls
from torchy throb full of mimicry
it is substance it wants to be object & so pretends
& keeps adding to itself & subtracting from same (with a difference)
the subduction pretending to accretion
as if anointing brow not acromion
as though it can penetrate subtly, subtly
pass into

Welcome back.

1

2

3

4

5

it's all fuzzy monologic.

lists of side effects float across
the wavering heated air.

(you know what I'm talking about, right, because that was so descriptive?)

my kitty cat feels a lot of them with me
because we have a supernatural disconnection
involving his white fur and my extremities.

where are the tranquillizers,
ourselves with homynyms,
esp. rich, riddle, and rifle.

I could go on but there are too many
and others better than I have listed them.

here's what I will say to him with my hands:
I was thinking about anger
and then a band of heat in my brain flared for a moment.

no, not that.

do I sound confused?

I sound confused even with no sound,
or I mean even with only certain sounds
of which I am not the source.

I won't say anything then.

nothing is happening.

nothing is ever happening when something something something what?

not wanting to use,
person is waiting.
not wanting to use I,
person is suggesting.
equation. create an equation.
when I think you,
word can see them.
"but" then wants to
seesaw, keeps wanting.
you can see me/them
meaning to touch your hair.
our poor hearing.
contact as a pivot.
draws some equals signs.
two letters nest in
this then mouth, see them then.
touching without point with
several words, type of myself.
"that is" and say "point"
while organs point in and out.
our poor wanty ears
go without saying.

public race to the moment the belt slides from its loops. it shapes it, its theories of itself

specify generic time of mass = x — you scratch the bump to make it become a bump.

this is the personal.

one passes time to become little. ending. space.

a person touches me (him/her) softly or painfully or does not touch me (him/her) ever.

& then as a passage the talkie room on the screen full of two bodies —

pure love deleted from the title: replaced with glove.

*perihelion*

the picnic is set, desires aroused and written on the cake — as of
wanting to care for others badly

in the them of home and other alcoholic teacher Protestant agnostics —
experiencing arousal
         from a safe so-it-seems
      distance

causing them to tremble along someone else's mandible — summer
language in use to break
          up the speech
        picnic

as though anything of this had a moral equivalence — in some
recherché rollover fill-in-the-blank
         sovereign idea of haters

circulating porcelain sleep — made vulnerable by the utter lostness only
impossible on a screen

the butterknife locked in the basement with token pianos, an infancy —
creating a palpable air
         of disease

each type of mouth toys with crumbs and boats — wailing on the dais
for clutching smallness as
        hard as it shakes
        them

using esoteric tools for treating the tense face esoterically — in the shape of needles driving

                                                numbly through pieces of
                                                body

they were akin to highbrow speeches and lowbrow speeches — brick in the eye, falls and fires,

                                          several burnings windowed at
                                different times

the red and yellow curtains turning to fires — other black buildings to terrify the town with final

                                                  accidents

being chided for speaking and sighing yet no one asked why are they crying — if there were a

                                        room that could name the also
                                        others

the glass in their necks happened to form a little hot warmth — water flowing from the brain,

                                                    onions for
                                                    eyes

during summer dressed as winter & its analysis — hoping the stanching stanches with pariahs,

                                        homonyms, phones and
                                      horses

why fire always comes to it, as a question thought and not said by the smaller ones — such

                                            shaking as happened
                                to them

black kite on the pavement, grunting of a cat, a type of monster—
hearing a creature sigh
                                                        through their
                                        pinkies

words last to score the tongue as the backfires badly show—breathing
clicks into their fat
                              hearts, diverted from clogged and
                                                    spacious
                                            vessels

space, scar, stimulus, semi-cruelty—burning retinas into acceptable
patterns, reforming silence
                                        can unname itself, pass
                                        across

rising in an unmarked unsaid mammal anger—no surface to be under,
moons regret
                                                  through
                                          phrases

the embouchure, the elements rushing through—how many scaffolds
bespoke terror
                                                  into their sleeves for comfort

having chosen a phoneme to debase themselves—as though in being
this dream they're the
                                          opposite of
                                something

spread over the course of a body—it was the accidental windows on
fire inside them

Welcome back.

1

2

3

4

5

6

7

8

9

10

11

making pause for a soft cuss at your earth.

that sounds kind of sexy
but isn't meant to be.

the hive is full and sleeping now.

what is that shape of that sound
off to that periphery.

it would be a lifelong project to know —
or I would have to be a different person,
or just accept whatever.

holding my body with my body
as though it used to be a glass
full of water.
it may have been the partially angry water
returning as gone.

but maybe the glass is very large and very empty
and you can see things through it,
like a sky and some trees.

things are getting sketchy that were already sketchy on the sky,
cloudish, nightish, owlish,
a black plane.

everything seems drawn —
you seem drawn.

involuntary darkening of face,
room,
        block,
                town.

there is no concept.

there just isn't.

*pantograph*

shame scrawled with jelly — over the lunette

our grove of somewhat trees that gave of figs — beneath the lunette

one in the popular book with a traumatized head, eternal urination, root killing — viewed through the lunette

pubic brain hair duct-taped — across the lunette

incarnational daughtership — blearing the lunette

injury as uselessly timeless path adhesed to leaving — in the shadow of the lunette

from this our object

through which birdsong turned to pressure in the torso up to face tingling

                    wee on our tippy toes

*aphelion*

ev ery sleep comes at once v ia ava lanche of sleep ing men cry snow
flakes stain less

cheek calc ulates eye count it in your pores the velo city smoothes into
cries

cast a type of play with no charac ters only a ffliction- for ged
graphemes e nough white space

to crawl out of fee ling serif s draw blood also f aintly feel ing others feel
them du ring the crawl
up. ward.

for these mater ials that I have which are l oad bearing res ting res ting
over by the way side

that tear ful state red me tal s hells that one mel ts be fore drink ing
pronouns among which
pr onouns rotate to con trol the birthing cham ber

rest ing rest ing over by the way side thinning to night mare such very
little sun spot swarm in
carun cula

name ly the cries do have ways of putting a tem poral app aratus to m
ultiverse of bitte r lovey
gho sty thoughts

or other wise that fall int o the small you held alpha be tically
I think the me that you are to me feigns fear at the man ner of teles
copes the mselves

some or igins mutely ass ert them selves conti nue a par allel structure
sm older on the fire
es cape of ear as a tear drop bery l

the plan kton frozen plant and an imal tee ming in muscula r drifts
might call it em erald as ick and is
and care and force fuse mom entarily

aw aiting neck scent pro ximity or feed thirst y on cold me tallic flow ers
every yellow cor d breaks the
s triving into fin gers they grow out o f

as I sit and breathe grow mode rat e as I sit and breathe keep co ming
back and sayin g that
and to uching gen tly the sayi ng of it back

*acknowledgments*

I would like to acknowledge the following editors for publishing work from this book: Rebecca Wolf at *Fence*; E. Tracy Grinnell at *Aufgabe*; Anselm Berrigan at *Brooklyn Rail*; Stacy Szymaszek at *The Recluse*; Maureen Thorson at *Open Letters Monthly*; and Katie Fuller at *Stolen Island*. Gratitude goes to my wonderful UDP people, Matvei Yankelevich, Emmalea Russo, and Anna Moschovakis. And thanks to the DC poets, to Nancy and Richard, to Monkey and Macho, and to Sasha and Ken, most of all most of all.

*about the author*

Cathy Eisenhower lives and works as a therapist in Washington, DC, and is the author of *Language of the Dog-heads* (Phylum, 2001), *clearing without reversal* (Edge, 2008), and *would with and* (Roof, 2009). She is co-translating the selected poems of Argentine poet Diana Bellessi and co-curated the In Your Ear Reading Series for several years. Her work has recently appeared in *The Recluse, Aufgabe, West Wind Review, The Brooklyn Rail,* and *Fence.*

*colophon*

This book was printed in an edition limited to 1400 at McNaughton & Gunn in Saline, Michigan. It was designed by good utopian. The text and titles are set in Scala.